YOU AND ME
9 TO 90
YEARS

GAURAV PATHAK

About the Author

The author of this book is Gaurav Pathak, born on 23rd June 1995 in Hazaribagh, a city in Jharkhand. He completed his schooling up to class 12th in Jaipur and then moved to Amity University, Noida, for his graduation. Currently, he resides in Delhi with his family.

Dedication

To my girlfriend, the most beautiful and genuine person I know:

I dedicate this book to you with all my heart. Through these pages, I hope to express my deepest apologies for my mistakes and seek your forgiveness. Your grace and understanding mean the world to me, and I am truly sorry for any pain I have caused.

This book is also a tribute to my father, a renowned author, whose influence and encouragement have inspired me since childhood. It has always been my dream to write, and I am grateful to finally have the chance to share my words, thanks to his legacy.

The cover painting is a gift from Kaira, a beautiful work of art that she created for me. I hope to honor her in the next series with her name and permission.

Introduction

This is a story of Gautam and Kaira, two souls deeply in love. Their journey began on a college trip, where they first met, and on April 16, 2015, their bond blossomed into a relationship. Their love for each other was undeniable, and together, they dreamt of a future hand in hand.

From planning their lives together to preparing for government jobs, they supported each other through every step. Their journey took them through many places as they moved forward, sharing dreams and challenges. Starting from Amity University, their story unfolds, revealing the joys, struggles, and hopes they shared.

As you turn the pages of this book, you will discover what happened in their lives, how their paths intertwined, and what the future holds for them. The full story awaits you within these pages.

Chapter 1.

No train stops at this station except for a passenger train at 9:00 AM. Every night from 2:00 AM to 4:00 AM, you wait for a train. A drunkard named Suresh asked Gautam this question. Suresh was always found lying there, drunk, every night. He noticed that Gautam would arrive at the tracks at 1:00 AM and sit in front of them, doing nothing but staring intently at the passing trains—goods trains, Rajdhani Express, and others. He would just watch them closely without saying a word. He would occasionally glance at his mobile and then leave for home at 4:00 AM. Suresh found this behaviour very strange.

Suresh often asked Gautam to drink with him, saying, "Just have a little, and tell me, where are you going? Which train are you waiting for?"

But Gautam never answered. He would simply take out a cigarette from his pocket, finish an entire pack throughout the night, and continue sitting there.

One day, Gautam saw a train approaching at high speed and began to walk towards it. Seeing this, Suresh thought perhaps this was the train Gautam had been waiting for, the one that would take him to his destination. But what happened next was something entirely different. Gautam walked directly in front of the train, ready to step onto the tracks. At that moment, Suresh, despite being drunk, felt all his intoxication vanish. He ran towards Gautam and pushed him away from the tracks, saving him from the train.

Gautam screamed in a loud voice, "I had finally found my destination! Why did you make me miss my train? I won't reach my destination with a drunkard like you!"

Suresh helped him up and said, "Listen, whatever is troubling you, speak about it. If you keep such things buried inside, there's no solution to be found. Tell me what's on your mind."

Gautam broke down, crying as if he had been hiding a deep pain for a long time. Suresh led him to the other side of the station where construction work was going on. He sat him down behind a truck, offered him some water, and said, "Sir, everyone in this world has some sorrow; everyone is fighting their own battles. If we don't share our grief, it will consume us. So, whatever it is that's bothering you, tell me. You seem like an educated and decent person. What happened that made you think like this?"

In a soft voice, Gautam said, "I have committed a murder."

Upon hearing this, Suresh felt his hands and feet go cold. He worried that he might be in the company of a criminal who could harm him. But the pain in Gautam's eyes suggested that he wasn't someone who would harm anyone. So Suresh asked, "Whose murder did you commit? Tell me now."

Gautam needed someone who wouldn't judge him, and he felt that Suresh, being drunk, might be that person. In a very soft voice, Gautam said, "I murdered my fiancée's trust."

Suresh looked at him closely, then laughed and said, "Oh, so this is a matter of love!"

Gautam remained silent.

Chapter 2

Suresh knew that Gautam's mental state wasn't stable and that if he left him alone, he might do something drastic. Despite Gautam's repeated refusals, Suresh forced him to come to his house. When Gautam arrived, he saw a broken mat, a charpoy, and a water pot. Suresh's financial situation was clearly not good.

Suresh asked Gautam, "What do you do, sir?"

In a very low voice, Gautam replied, "I'm a government employee."

Suresh looked at him and said, "Then if your son had a life-threatening disease, you could probably save him, right?"

Gautam didn't understand and asked, "What do you mean?"

Suresh, in a very soft voice, said, "Nothing much, first tell me, why were you on the tracks, and why do you come to the station every night?"

He placed his hand on Gautam's shoulder and said, "I'm here with you, so go ahead and tell me."

Gautam broke down and started crying, saying through his tears, "I've ruined my happy life. I love her so much, more than anything."

Suresh had already sensed that the situation was serious. He gave Gautam some water and said, "The night is long. Whatever is on your mind, just let it out."

Gautam had no one to talk to, so he thought maybe sharing his story would lighten his burden. He decided to tell Suresh his story.

"It was on February 21, 2015, when I first met her. She was wearing a kurti with the word 'Gucci' written on it. She kept pushing her hair back as if it was bothering her. She had a mole under her lip, which I thought protected her from all evil eyes. She stood there in quiet simplicity. My friend, Roshni, introduced me to her with a slight smile, saying, 'Gautam, this is Kaira, and she is joining us on our trip to Mathura.'

I forgot to mention earlier, we were going on a college trip to Mathura, and I found out a day before that Kaira would be joining us. I first met her that morning at the college gate. She smiled warmly at me and said hello. I was lost in her beauty, simplicity, and innocence. Looking at her, my heart kept telling me that she was way out of my league. But who could explain that to my heart?

Our trip to Mathura began. We had rented two cars for the trip. Kaira was in the other car, and I was in the first one. After a short distance, we decided to stop at a place to grab something to eat. When I went ahead to check on the car, I saw that one of my car's tires was punctured. As I was driving the car to get the tire fixed, I saw Kaira standing nearby with one of my friends, buying some stuff. Seeing her, I became so nervous that I forgot why I was there and what I wanted to do. She was standing just a few steps away, where everyone was sitting and eating. In my nervousness, I couldn't say much, so I just told her, 'I'll get the tire fixed and then drop you back.'

She smiled and said, 'Yes, it's quite a distance from here to where I'm standing with the others,' and then she laughed. That one smile gave me a happiness I had never felt before, and I kept thinking about it and smiling until we reached Mathura.

We visited a temple there. It's said that whatever you wish for at the temple comes true. A priest asked me for a donation, and I gave him a small amount. He then told me that I would only find fulfilment when I find my other half. I jokingly told him, 'I'm alone; where will I find my other half?' Little did I know that God had already decided to make me complete.

We kept exploring various places in Mathura, and then someone in our group suggested that we should try some bhang. Her friends even asked her if she wanted to try some, but she shook her head very innocently and declined. Her refusal won my heart. In this day and age, I didn't think there were still girls like her. I've always believed that intoxication is bad for both boys and girls, but seeing her refuse when everyone else was eager to try it really impressed me. But winning my heart wasn't enough; I had to win hers.

Our day-long trip was coming to an end, and it was around 9:00 PM when we finally returned to the college gate. She had fallen asleep in the car. One of her friends called out to her, 'Wake up, Kaira, we're back at the college.' With her beautiful, innocent look, she slowly pushed her hair back with her hands and softly said, 'I want to sleep more.' I prayed to God that I could hear that line every morning for the rest of my life.

I returned to my room, physically present, but my heart was left behind somewhere. That much I knew."

Chapter 3

February 21st was over, and February 22nd had begun. I woke up at 6:00 AM, still half-asleep, and immediately called Roshni.

"Roshni, I need your help. How do I talk to her? Does she have a boyfriend?" I was nervously crossing my fingers, hoping for a "No." She yelled back, "Do you even realize what time it is? It's 6:00 in the morning! Is this the time to talk about such things?"

But how could I explain to her that when someone is in love, time doesn't matter? Only the person they love does. I apologised, laughing, "Sorry, I disturbed you. How about this: I'll treat you to a party in college today. Just tell me what you know."

She understood that I had lost my heart. Laughing, she replied, "Good news for you—she's single."

Relieved, I asked, "Roshni, do you have any ideas on how I can talk to her, how I can bring her closer, and how I can get to know her better?"

That day, I realised that a lover in love could deceive anyone. The next morning, we had an exam. Abhishek and I had already planned to sit together during the exam so we could help each other out. But when I reached the class, Roshni came up to me and said, "Gautam, if you sit next to me and help me pass the paper, I'll try to get her to accept your friend request on Facebook today."

I immediately rushed to sit next to Roshni, leaving Abhishek stunned. He teased me with the classic college line, "Got a girl and forgot your friends, huh? Remember, one day you'll be back with your buddies." But I didn't care about anything else; all I could see was that if she accepted my Facebook request, maybe I could finally talk to her.

That evening, Roshni sent me a video where she was recording Kaira viewing my Facebook profile. Seeing that brought me such immense joy that I can't describe it. I treated two or three people to ice cream at my PG. They asked why I was celebrating, and I simply said, "I'm just feeling good."

As I got closer to my goal, she accepted my Facebook request the next day. Seeing that, I sent a very lame and boring message: "Thank you for accepting my request."

The following day, I received a message saying, "You're welcome." It's true what they say—school and college friends are irreplaceable. It wasn't just me trying to win her over; all my friends were helping too, including Shubham, Roshni, Abhishek, and even some of her friends. It felt like I was fighting a battle, but with everyone on my side, it was much easier.

The next morning, I heard that Farhan Akhtar was coming to perform at our college. I told Roshni to bring her to the show. "You come too; the four of us will hang out, and maybe I'll get to talk to her," I said. She agreed, and I was excited, though I complained, "Three days is a long time! Who knows what could happen in three days?"

Roshni just smiled and said, "You're already feeling that three days is too long?". The next day Roshni Said that Kaira is not feelimh well. I panicked when I heard that she wasn't feeling well. I started searching the internet for remedies for a cold and found one where you tie camphor in a cloth to help fight the cold. I quickly prepared it and handed it to

Roshni, telling her, "Give this to her; it'll make her feel better."

After two long days of waiting, Farhan Akhtar's show finally arrived. She appeared in a white shirt, blue jeans, slightly damp hair, and blue shoes. Her smile was still the same, shy and beautiful. I think she was more shy around me than I was around her. Shubham asked, "Want anything to eat?" but my throat was too dry to respond. This happened so many times.

Farhan Akhtar started performing live, and we were all watching him. I was frustrated with myself for not knowing how to whistle. Shubham was whistling loudly, and she kept turning around to look at him. I wished it was me she was looking at instead. I even joked with Shubham, "Next time, I'll pretend to whistle, and you can whistle for real from behind so she thinks it's me."

The entire function ended, and she was about to leave when she suddenly turned to me and said, "Gautam, thank you so much for the camphor. It actually helped." I was in shock, unable to respond. Roshni gestured for me to say something, and Shubham urged me too. But by the time I gathered the courage to speak, she was already gone.

I quickly ran after her and her friends and said to Kaira Wait Gautam wants to say something, I had nothing much to say. I just said "thank you for accepting my Facebook request." And with that, our conversation ended. Slowly, she had taken over my heart and mind, but I had no idea what was happening to me. I couldn't eat unless I received a message from her. I couldn't get out of bed in the morning until I saw her online status on Facebook. I was completely lost in her, day and night, dreaming about her.

One day, I gathered all my courage and asked her, "Could I have your number? I'm not always online on Facebook, but if I had your number, I could message you directly on WhatsApp when I need to."

I was scared that she might say no, so I didn't open Facebook all night. The next morning, when I finally did, there it was—her number. It felt like I had won a Nobel Prize. I got out of bed, put on a special perfume, picked out new clothes, and walked with a newfound confidence, feeling like the luckiest person in the world.

When I reached college, I couldn't focus on anything but her number. In the botany class, I kept repeating it in my head. The teacher noticed that I was lost and asked, "Gautam, what are we discussing in class?"

Of course, I had no idea. She kicked me out of class, but even outside, all I could think about was whether she would be nearby.

Now, the time had come to take things further. My entire gang was involved. There were five of us: me, Shubham, Roshni, Abhishek, and Om Prakash. Everyone except Om Prakash wanted me to be in a relationship with her. Om Prakash didn't like me and had even warned Roshni several times not to introduce her to me, threatening that he would cheat if she did. But Roshni didn't listen and did everything she could to bring us together.

Following Shubham's plan, we all planned another trip, this time to Rishikesh. I was sure she wouldn't refuse and would be ready to go. So, we started making all the arrangements—booking hotels, deciding on the adventure activities, everything. She was ready, and I was ready. We were all very excited for the trip. My plan was to propose to her in Rishikesh. I believed that this trip would change my life forever.

Chapter 4

Finally, that was all we did when we were about to start our journey. Before starting, in college, people had to get a gate pass for night outs, which required parental permission. Now, it's obvious that parents wouldn't easily give you permission, so this trip was kept secret from everyone, and we had to leave at night. I remember that night well; I saw a different side of her, a carefree, little girl who wanted to enjoy her college life differently. She wanted to live like a free bird, without any restrictions, and on her terms. But at that time, I couldn't fully understand her.

We decided to go to Shubham's flat. We took an auto and reached there, where everyone was already gathered. I was just observing her, and whenever she looked at me, I would look away, pretending not to notice her. It was Shivaratri, and I had told her that I would also fast, but I'm not very good at keeping fasts. I couldn't resist the temptation to eat when I saw food, so I couldn't keep the fast for long, but she was determined.

The next morning, she had to go to the temple with one of her friends. She had already planned it, and I was a bit disappointed that I couldn't go with her, but I was happy that at least she was going. We decided that since there wasn't enough space in the flat, Abhishek and I would return to our place, while Roshni and her friends stayed there, and Shubham went to stay with another friend.

Around 2 AM, there was a power cut at their place. Roshni called Shubham, saying they were scared because there was no electricity. Shubham immediately went there on his scooter, picked them up, and took them to another flat where he was staying. Shubham later told me that this was Kaira's first night out, and she was so happy, like she had found something new. She was looking at everything outside the auto with such excitement, enjoying the whole night out on the road.

When you go to college, you dream of living your life freely, away from your parents' protective environment. It's not that their protection is wrong, but everyone craves freedom, and experiencing it brings a different kind of joy. That's what Kaira was feeling too. The next morning, when I found out that they had changed their location during the night, I got a bit upset. I started scolding Shubham, saying, "Don't you have any sense? How could you take them to a new place at that time? What if something had happened? You should be more careful." Shubham tried to calm me down, saying,

"Relax, Gautam, we won't let anything happen to Kaira. We were just having fun." I eventually calmed down.

The next day, we started our journey to Rishikesh. Everyone was excited. However, due to some reasons, Kaira and I couldn't sit in the same car. She was with her friends, and I didn't want to make her uncomfortable, so I sat in a different car. But I was constantly getting updates about her from Roshni – what Kaira was doing, what she was saying. Slowly, we reached Rishikesh.

We had booked a camp near the Ganges. The way from where we parked our car to the camp was like descending a steep mountain. I had noticed earlier that Kaira was afraid of heights, so I looked at Roshni and, gathering all my courage, offered my hand to Kaira. Without a second thought, she took my hand. As we descended, she tightened her grip whenever the path got difficult. It felt like I was lost, unaware of where we were going or how the path was. All I knew was that I was holding her hand, and that gave me immense joy. We finally reached our camp, where it was quite dark, with only dim lights here and there.

Later, everyone planned to sit by the Ganges, outside the camp, and have some beer. This was the first trip for everyone, and we wanted to enjoy it in our way. We were all sitting together – Shubham, Roshni, Kaira's friend, and I. Someone opened a beer bottle, and everyone looked at me. I had told Kaira earlier that I don't drink, but I was always so nervous around her that I couldn't react normally. I thought maybe if I drank, I'd be more relaxed around her, so I agreed to have some beer. But Kaira was firm in her decision; once she said no, she didn't touch the alcohol.

Everyone else drank except Kaira. After a few drinks, we were all a bit tipsy. Roshni, trying to have some fun, teased Kaira, saying, "Gautam has set your picture as his wallpaper." Kaira didn't like it at all; I could tell by her expression that she was annoyed. She got up and went inside her tent. I realized that maybe she didn't have any feelings for me. Sitting there, I thought that there might not be any possibility between us. If she was so open about her feelings, it probably meant she didn't have any for me. I had mistaken her kindness for affection.

I knew she was out of my league; she could easily find someone much better than me. I quietly went to sleep, feeling dejected. But the next morning, when I saw her in her orange and grey top, all the negativity from the previous night vanished. Maybe she was just in a bad mood last night, I thought.

Maybe she does have some feelings for me. With a renewed sense of hope, we started our day.

We bathed in the Ganges and then went for rafting. Kaira and her friends were in a playful mood, trying to get lifts from bikers just for fun. Initially, it annoyed me, but then I realized that they were just having fun, which is a part of life. We then set off for rafting, navigating the Ganges. At one point, a huge wave almost overturned our raft, and four out of the eight people in our boat fell into the water. I immediately looked back and saw that Kaira was still in the raft, and that gave me such a sense of relief.

During the rafting, there was a moment when Kaira and I ended up face-to-face in the water. We smiled at each other, and that moment was captured in a group photo. I later cropped that photo to make it a personal one of just the two of us. After rafting, we found a puppy with a bandaged leg. I saw Kaira petting it lovingly, and it is said that those who love animals have a good heart. I witnessed that firsthand as she gently stroked the puppy, which seemed to adore her back. She always named the animals she met, but I didn't get the chance to ask what she named this one.

Due to time constraints, we couldn't do much else, except for rafting and enjoying a bonfire by the Ganges at night. Our return journey began around 10 PM. My eyes searched for Kaira everywhere. She was in another car, wearing a black top. I caught glimpses of her, and every time, I felt like I was witnessing a masterpiece created with utmost care.

The drive back was tiring, and since we hadn't slept the night before, I started dozing off while driving. At one point, I lost control and hit the car in front of us. Our car was damaged, but thankfully, everyone was safe. Kaira was in the car behind us. After the accident, everyone moved to the other car, and we started changing the tire that had burst.

Roshni messaged me from the other car, saying, "Don't worry, Kaira is really concerned about you." Hearing that, all my worries vanished. Roshni added, "She's saying that Gautam looks so tired and stressed; he hasn't slept properly." Hearing that, it felt like Kaira was genuinely concerned about me, and what started as a negative experience turned into a positive one.

The accident ended up costing me around 15-16 thousand rupees. But my college friends were great; they said, "It was your mistake, but we'll all contribute." So, everyone chipped in about 1500 each, and the expense was shared. We finally reached the flat from where our journey had begun.

This journey had ended, but I hadn't yet managed to propose to Kaira in Rishikesh. Yet, I felt a strange unease, like I was losing someone close to me. I didn't know when we'd get another chance to spend so much time together again. There was a lingering fear in my heart, but I knew she was still in the same college, and I was too. So, I returned home, and Kaira went back to her home. My father was posted in Jaipur, and Kaira's father was in Kota.

We continued chatting on WhatsApp. She was replying, and that kept our conversation going. One day, I decided that we should meet alone. Summoning all my courage, I asked Kaira, and she gave a positive reply, saying, "Okay, message me whenever you're free. If I'm free, we'll meet." For me, that was a huge ray of hope. I waited eagerly for the day we'd meet alone, and I could finally tell her what was in my heart.

Chapter 5

The day had finally arrived when I was supposed to meet Kaira. She had already left her home. Her train had departed from Kota at 5:00 AM and was expected to arrive at Nizamuddin Railway Station at 12:35 PM. I had meticulously searched through all the trains to confirm which one she would be on. At exactly 2:20 PM, I messaged her, "Hey, Kaira, I'm free today. If possible, can we meet at 4:30 PM? Please respond positively." She agreed and said she would meet me near H Block. We both decided to meet near our college, where there had been an accident. I still remember she was walking ahead of me, on her way to meet me, while I followed behind. Her hand was bandaged, possibly from an injury at home. When I first saw her, she was wearing a pink top, blue denim jeans, and white printed slippers. She was walking ahead with a brown bag in her hand. As usual, when she came in front of me, I lost myself in the moment, unaware of how I was even walking.

When I realized she was about to reach H Block, I hurried to catch up with her. As soon as I arrived, she smiled beautifully and said, "Hi." I responded with a smile and then we both sat down. There was silence between us because I was shy, and she was equally shy. She would sometimes look up at the ceiling or glance to the side, but whenever she spoke, her voice and tone were unlike anything I had ever heard. After a while, I asked, "Would you like something?" She replied, "Coffee." and insisted on paying, but since it was my first time with a girl, I couldn't let her pay. I suggested, "How about this—I'll pay this time, and you can pay next time." We both smiled at this. I went to get coffee, and as it was our first meeting, I knew she liked chocolate, so I quickly ran to a nearby departmental store and bought a dark chocolate bar for her. She initially said she couldn't accept it, and for a moment, I thought she wouldn't take it and refused. When I was alone with her, talking to her, she kept pushing her hair behind her ears, but they would keep falling forward. I noticed one thing about her: whenever she drank something, she would press it tightly with her teeth, leaving marks on the cup. She was so shy and nervous. We sat there for about an hour and a half, and then we left.

The entire night, I kept thinking that if I continued to be this shy, I would never be able to express myself in front of her. I wondered if I could ever bring her into my life or if I would just keep having these normal conversations. On the other hand, Roshni used to tell me that there was another guy who was trying to get close to her. I knew that anyone would want someone like her in their life, and I felt I wasn't even worthy of being compared to them. This thought troubled me deeply. I knew that many handsome and well-educated boys would be pursuing her, and I felt that my chances were slim. But I was still fighting for that one percent chance, hoping that maybe, just maybe, she would fall in love with me too.

Whenever she was in front of me, I couldn't say what I wanted to say. I got so nervous. I also noticed that whenever I wore nice clothes to college, hoping to run into her, she would never show up. But on the days when I was dressed poorly, she would always appear. I would sit there, frustrated, thinking, "When will my luck turn? When will I be able to talk to her properly? When will I be able to tell her how I feel?"

At one point, I even thought of taking something that would make me say everything on my mind, but I never went that far. Our conversations on WhatsApp continued normally. After three or four days, I asked her again if we could meet on a Saturday. Her friends were all going out to eat, but she couldn't refuse me. She said, "Okay, you can come." On Saturdays, the college gates were closed, and I had a hard time getting inside. Later, I found out that she had told her friends that her mom was coming, even though her mom was actually arriving in the evening. She stayed back just to meet me, and this meant a lot to me—she had turned down her friends to stay back for me. I was smiling to myself, wondering if I deserved this. My eyes welled up with tears because she had done so much for me.

We met again near H Block, where we had met before, but Kaira's roommate was standing there. Kaira then suggested that we go somewhere else since she wanted to keep her personal life private and didn't want her roommate to see us together. At that time, we were not yet certain about what we were to each other. We went to a restaurant called Wall Street and ordered noodles and chilli potatoes. I noticed how lovingly she ate the noodles and chilli potatoes, even though she was nervous. She mixed the two together and ate them slowly. I asked her, "Roshni told me that you all were planning to go out to eat today." She replied, "Yes, but my mom is coming soon." I said, "Okay, let's finish up quickly then, so your mom doesn't worry." But she wasn't good at lying, and during our conversation, she let it slip that her mom would arrive at 5:00 PM. That made me realise she had only stayed back to meet me, using her mom as an excuse to her friends.

I felt that she was an amazing person who couldn't break anyone's heart. After we met, I went back home and found myself smiling again, humming the song, "Is this love? Yes, this is love." If someone hasn't fallen in love yet, they might not understand the meaning of that song. Love is a feeling, a magical thing that you only understand once you've experienced it. When you're in love, you forget everything else. The only thing you see in front of you is that person. You just want to be with them. You lose sleep, peace, and control over your life, as your entire life becomes centred around that one person. I had lost control over my life.

Then came the time for bargaining with God. I started making deals with God, saying things like, "If she becomes my girlfriend, I'll do this," or "If she becomes my girlfriend, I'll do that." I began feeding poor children, hoping for blessings that would bring her into my life. I tried everything I could think of.

Then came the day, April 15th. I called her, and we had planned to meet that day. Before meeting her, with Roshni's help, I had created a collage of her childhood to recent photos, and I planned to give it to her on April 15th. While preparing this collage I shared with roshni that I want to write a novel on your love story, if it gets successful. Roshni laughed and said you guys will make amazing pair she is also planning to write a novel on deaf childrens. I was actually thinking our hobbies are same. But sometimes, things don't go as planned. When I called her on April 15th, she cut my call and messaged, "We can't meet today, I'm busy." What had happened? I had put in so much effort, and yet, I was left feeling dejected. Roshni was watching me and asked, "What happened?" I said, "She refused to meet." I felt like crying in the library, but I controlled my tears. I went home, determined not to give up, and messaged her, "I had something for you. I was hoping we could meet." She agreed to meet on April 16th.

On April 16th, I arrived with a black bag she didn't like. I called it a "drum bag," but she taught me it was called a "duffel bag." I showed her the collage I had made, and she smiled beautifully while looking at it. During this time, I realized I had forgotten to mention something—Kaira had a sad past, she had been in love with a boy who had broken her heart by getting into a relationship with someone else. She was still carrying the pain from that relationship, which I could see in her eyes. Roshni had already told me about this. Coincidentally, I had a friend named Shefali who studied at the same college as Kaira's ex-boyfriend. I asked her about him, and she told me he was very happy in a new relationship, doing well, and even sharing clothes with his new partner. After hearing this, I felt that

Kaira deserved the happiness she was missing, and I wanted to be the one to give it to her.

When I gave Kaira the collage, I told her that I was going to say something that might shake her world. And then, in a fraction of a second, Kaira asked me, "Can we get into a relationship today?" I was taken aback. I wasn't prepared for this. I asked her again, "Are you serious?" I couldn't say anything. My world was spinning. I didn't know what was happening. Was this real? Was she really going to be my girlfriend? I couldn't believe it. Everything felt like a dream. I saw a smile on Kaira's face, but I couldn't tell if it was real or fake. By then, she had already become my girlfriend.

After she became my girlfriend, I tried to shift from being a normal guy to acting like a boyfriend, but I couldn't. Our conversation ended in a minute because I had nothing more to say. April 16th was coming to an end, and it had been one of the biggest days of my life. I still couldn't believe what had happened. I was sitting quietly, looking at the ground, feeling incredibly innocent. I fell asleep with a smile on my face.

The next day, I was eagerly waiting to meet her at college.

Chapter 6

Before I knew it, the morning of April 17th had arrived. I had gone outside for some work and saw some grapes. Knowing that Kaira liked grapes a lot, I packed them for her. I knew she really liked them, so I called her and asked her to come over for a bit. She came, and when I gave her the bag of grapes, she gave me a sweet smile. Her face expressed everything she wanted to say to me. I didn't want to understand her feelings in the rain; I preferred to remain unaware because I thought the truth might be harsh. Now that she had said yes, I decided to continue as we were. It's a sign of a petty person, which I was and still am. If you truly love someone, you should first understand if that person loves you from the heart or not. I didn't even try to understand; I felt that since she had agreed, she came. I didn't pay any attention to why or how she agreed. In my mind, I just wanted to give her so much love that she would forget all her past sorrows and grievances.

But the difficulty is that if you don't love someone, you can't spend even a few minutes with them. She had been with me since last night, and she had planned to stay for an indefinite time, which I didn't know. However, she never once let me feel that she didn't love me. That evening, I received a call from her. I answered the call with great fear, thinking she might be calling to say that it wasn't working out between us. But instead, she asked me to come and meet her. I rushed over, and her friend was standing at the gate, smiling. She congratulated me, saying it was a big thing for her. She said If you ever deceived or left Kaira no one would be worse off than me. I assured her that I would never betray her. If I brought Kaira into my life, it was only to make her happy and fulfil all her wishes.

We celebrated our relationship in a grand manner, partying at a hotel. I felt great that we started our relationship at a new level. I always prayed to God that our relationship never faced any problems. I had already decided that I wanted to marry her and keep her happy forever. As the night went on, and morning arrived. After spending two minutes on the phone, we didn't realize how it turned into two hours. After one month of relationship We decided to thank Lord Krishna in Mathura. I had teased her many times about her never being on time. That day, to prove me wrong, she hadn't slept all night and came directly without sleeping. Her eyes showed it, but she was lying. We saw all of Mathura from the car; all the temples were closed. During the journey, she had slept on my hand. She was so tired that she lied about being awake, so she had to sleep in the car. We had coffee and jaljeera in

Mathura. The jaljeera was quite bad, but the best part was being with Kaira; I didn't need anything better. Later, we took our first photo on the highway. I was in a white shirt and she in her top. That was the best moment. For me, it still felt like a dream that had somehow come true. I was afraid that it might fall apart.

Kaira's way of loving was very different; she never let her problems show. She handled everything with a smile. She never made any demands or complaints, just arrived a bit late. The reason was that if we decided to meet at 4:30, I would arrive at 3:45. Whenever I said I had arrived, her only reaction was, "Okay, I'm coming." She didn't like waking up early but still came. One day, when I had arrived 30 minutes early, she asked why we couldn't stick to the decided time. I felt ashamed of it. Actually she always plans to take 30 mins nap before our decided time. But as she goes to bed. I calls her I am waiting outside. Before I could fix it, the college vacation time had come. It was a huge trauma for me to be without Kaira for two months, but I made a promise to visit Kota twice during those two months. The first time being away was very painful. Everything seemed pointless without Kaira. For the first time, I truly felt what it means when body and soul are not together.

Chapter 7

There was a peculiar fear within me—a fear whose origin I couldn't quite pinpoint. Perhaps it stemmed from my reluctance to ask Kaira if she harbored any doubts about our relationship. I would scrutinize her face, trying to decode any subtle expression that might reveal what she was truly feeling. Each night, I was haunted by the thought that she might slip away from me. The smallest delay of even ten minutes would send me spiraling into anxiety, imagining the worst. I would obsessively check to ensure she was okay, that everything was fine. My love for her was profound, so deep that the mere thought of being without her was unbearable. My patience was stretched thin, yet I tolerated everything for the sake of our love. If she didn't bid me goodnight or say "I love you," sleep would elude me. I'd wander through the night, restlessly awaiting the next morning's "good morning" to feel at peace again.

What was I so afraid of? Perhaps it was that unreadable expression on her face that planted seeds of doubt in my mind. But despite my fears, she never allowed me to feel abandoned.

When we talked on the phone at night, it felt as though we were invincible, bound together by something unbreakable. Yet, the moment she was away for more than an hour, worry would creep in—where could she be? One day, during a casual conversation, I mentioned that I had started a diary to chronicle our experiences, intending to gift it to her on her birthday. To my surprise, she revealed she had a similar plan. This shared thought process was a testament to the responsibilities we had taken on together.

On one occasion, I asked her if she thought about me for just ten minutes out of her entire day. I would cherish those ten minutes as if they were a whole day's worth of thoughts. Sometimes, I would ask how many hours she spent thinking of me, and though her answer never varied, one day she confessed that I occupied her thoughts for all twenty-four hours. It was clear—she was deeply in love with me.

In the beginning, when we were together without love for those initial 15-20 days, it was challenging. Pretending to love me when she didn't was difficult for her, yet she managed it with grace. On the first date of our relationship, she admitted that she had called her ex the night before, just to hear his voice, but she promised it would be the last time. I couldn't help but admire her honesty. However, this made me feel unworthy of her love, and the fear that I might lose such a wonderful person gnawed at me. This fear manifested as anxiety about her leaving, and I often wondered how I would survive without her. I was incomplete without her, and these thoughts drove me to create unnecessary tension in her life. I would bombard her with messages if she wasn't available for even an hour.

In my dreams, I often envisioned marrying her, imagining a future where we could proudly say we had been together for so long. They say that for a relationship to thrive, both partners must share similar thoughts and values. If one person is good and the other is not on the same level, the good one will suffer. To the world, she was a good person, but to me, she was exceptional. Her best friend didn't like me, which made me feel insecure, fearing that she might persuade Kaira to distance herself from me. Her friend believed I wasn't good enough for Kaira and wanted to keep us apart.

But Kaira, with her kind heart, could never hurt anyone's feelings. She assured me that she would talk less to her friend and meet me without her friend's knowledge. She didn't want to disappoint either of us. Yet, a small-minded person like myself couldn't fully grasp this, and it often left me feeling angry, though I couldn't express it.

The day finally came when we were to meet in Kota. From a distance, I saw her on a red scooter, wearing brown shades, an orange kurti, and black pajamas. In that moment, I questioned whether I truly deserved her. Instantly, I thought I wasn't worthy of her. When she handed me the keys to her scooter, it was as if she always wanted me to take the lead—a feeling I sensed from her actions. We watched a movie together, but I was so absorbed in her that I can't even remember the film. I consider it a great achievement that I managed to divert her attention from the movie to myself.

For my birthday, she gave me three letters and a white mug, which I wasn't sure how to use. As I was leaving after our meeting, a deep realisation struck me—I didn't want to lose her. I loved her beyond words; she was my life.

Chapter 8

The college break was over, and we were preparing to return. On the first day back, after the holidays, the hostel allotment was underway. Kaira was thinking that after so many days, everyone would have been hanging out with their friends, and she was returning to her room to relax with her family. Little did she know that she was harbouring a leech within her that fed on her blood. I called her with Aarti, asking her to speak with me. Some might say it was out of love, that I was overly attached and not respecting her space. I called her several times, concerned about her well-being, but she didn't pick up. After two hours, she finally replied, saying she was with her mother and would call me later.

Despite my attempts to understand her better, I kept pestering her, thinking she was just busy with friends and didn't want to spend time with me. It seemed like she was trying to balance her relationships with everyone, while I was self-centered. I was neglecting her feelings and focusing only on my own.

Over time, our relationship became increasingly toxic. I realised that despite claiming to love her deeply, I was only showing love in my own way, not considering her needs and desires. My approach was flawed; I was not respecting her individuality or understanding what made her happy. Instead of nurturing our relationship, I was trying to impose my own preferences and routines on her. I wanted her to fit into my life without considering what she truly wanted or needed.

Eventually, our once-sweet relationship deteriorated into a toxic one. Kaira's social life, which had been vibrant, faded as she focused on our relationship. My selfishness and lack of understanding led to this situation. I didn't respect her space or acknowledge her feelings, which gradually distanced her from her friends and led to a breakdown in her social relations.

In the end, I learned that genuine love is not about fulfilling your own desires but about understanding and accommodating your partner's needs. True love involves respecting and supporting each other, not just pursuing your own happiness. If you truly care for someone, you should prioritise their feelings and well-being over your own. Otherwise, you risk creating a relationship that only adds to their distress, rather than enriching their life.

Chapter 9

Gradually, month by month, our relationship progressed, and a strong bond formed between Kaira and me. I don't take credit for this; all the credit goes to Kaira. Life unfolded just the way I wanted, and we spent time together the way we wanted. Initially, we planned to spend just half an hour together after college, but that half-hour quickly turned into four hours without us even realising it. I don't even know when we started having lunch, breakfast, and dinner together. Maybe she wanted to do things with her friends, but I gradually stopped her from doing those things and made her start doing everything with me. She only went to the hostel to sleep; she did nothing else. She silently followed whatever I did, even though she didn't like sitting for hours in the H Block wasting time. But she did it because I wanted to.

Kaira crossed every limit in love; she became Juliet, but I could never become Romeo. This regret will always stay with me. I did love in my life, but on my own terms. And love done on one's own terms is not love; it's just selfishness. I didn't do anything for her happiness; everything was for my own happiness. But I didn't understand this at the time. By the time I realised it, it was too late. However,

Kaira never let this affect our relationship. She remained the same sweet and innocent girl who was always by my side, just as she had been before.

Now, the topic came up about taking our relationship forward. Kaira always wanted to go abroad for further studies. She was very focused and clear about her life goals—she wanted to do her Masters and Ph.D. abroad. That was her dream. On the other hand, I held on to an old-fashioned belief that after college, I should quietly prepare for a government job. My father had told me about the RBI Grade B Officer exam, and that was all I could think about. My mind knew it was a tough exam, but I thought that even if I could get any small government job, life would be set because of the facilities and benefits the government provides. But I never told kaira about this; I only talked about RBI Grade B and SBI PO with her. Kaira didn't like the idea of a bank job, though she liked the idea of an RBI job.

Slowly, I started convincing her. As I mentioned before, Kaira was initially on a different path, but gradually, I managed to steer her towards government job preparation, just like me, without her even realising it. She also started dreaming of a government job, but for only one reason: me. She took steps towards a government job only because I encouraged her to. We both joined a coaching institute named TIMES for preparation. We thought that by the time we reached our final year, we would have secured jobs.

I am a below-average-looking person, with nothing special to boast about. I don't have good looks, speaking skills, writing skills, or anything to be proud of. Kaira wanted to make me a better person, develop a good sense of dressing in me. She took care of all my clothing, but as they say, you can't change someone's core nature. Even though she got me good clothes, I would wear them without ironing them, which disappointed her. She would sometimes tell me to hit the gym and take care of my body. I would go to the gym for four days, and then go back to my old ways on the fifth day.

I would justify it by saying, "I love you so much, that's why I'm here outside your hostel." But if I truly loved her, I would have been doing these things for her, not for myself. I wasn't going to the hostel for her, I was going for myself because it was an easy way to avoid my responsibilities. If I truly loved her, I would have been building my body in the gym, trying to be a better person, speaking well, studying well, and trying to improve myself. But instead, I was just making excuses to spend time with her, and in the process, I disappointed her in every way possible, while she fulfilled every single thing I wanted.

Gradually, it wasn't just about keeping her away from friends; it extended to her family as well. Whenever she went home, I would message her to come back early because I missed her, and she started coming back earlier from home. She sacrificed everything for me, like lifting the weight of seven seas with one finger. kaira was like that; she wanted me to have a good body, look good, speak well, and have a good personality. These things didn't matter to me. If someone truly loves you, these things shouldn't matter, right? But by the time I realized this, it was too late.

kaira was like a saint, with no malice, deceit, or negativity in her. She always cared more about others' happiness than her own. Even today, I wonder if there are still girls like kaira in this world, and if there are, do I deserve them? Perhaps, I am just a narcissist who only thinks about himself and never about others.

kaira was the opposite of me; she always kept a reality check on herself and wanted me to do the same. But I often misunderstood her reality checks and argued with her. If someone truly loves you, they will point out your flaws because they want you to improve, not leave you. But I never understood that, and I kept making demands from her.

Time passed, and college life moved on. We enjoyed a lot of things together. We planned our future, talked about how we would live our lives, and our relationship was going well because kaira was very adjusting. She adjusted everything for me without complaining. But I kept taking her for granted, thinking, "If she's agreeing to this, she'll agree to that too." Sometimes, she would get angry, but she never expressed it openly. She would just ask me to leave her alone for a while to cool down, but I wouldn't let her. I would insist on talking and resolving the fight before going to bed. If things escalated, I would start crying to get her to forgive me.

If someone is crying in front of you, you can't help but feel bad. And I used my tears to manipulate her many times, asking for forgiveness. Maybe it didn't seem like much at the time, but these things accumulate over time and turn into frustration. kaira never let this show, but deep down, it must have been building up. She never let any negativity come to the surface, so I always thought she didn't have any. But maybe she did because she was human too.

Chapter 10

During our college days, we both had a strong desire to travel. However, since I had distanced myself from the group, and in the process, ended up isolating Kaira as well, we no longer had the option to travel together. Our parents would not have allowed us to go anywhere alone, so being part of a group was essential. As a result, I inadvertently hindered Kaira's dream of traveling. If we had a group, perhaps we could have planned a trip together. In my entire college life, I only managed to go on one trip to Rishikesh. Toward the end, by a stroke of luck, we found two people to accompany us to Manali.

As my college days were coming to an end in the third year, Kaira still had one more year left to complete her four-year B.Tech course. My fear at this point was that if I distanced myself from Kaira, it might affect our relationship. Kaira, who genuinely loved me, once suggested that I move to Rajendra Nagar to focus on my studies for a government job. She said she would visit me on Sundays, ensuring that my studies wouldn't suffer. Perhaps she thought that being away from me might help me focus, but I couldn't imagine being away from her. I couldn't bear the thought of being apart, thinking that distance might weaken our love. We were so accustomed to each other's presence that I couldn't imagine a life without her.

In contrast, Kaira was more practical and selfless. She was always thinking about what was best for me. She knew that if I studied hard for a year and secured a good job, our future would be secure. But I was stubborn. I kept telling her that I couldn't handle the distance and needed to be near her.

Our college had a placement cell, and I was keen to participate because I wanted a job in Delhi, where Kaira lived. Without her, everything seemed bleak to me. Even though I wanted to be with her all the time, she had the strength to focus on what was important for our future, while I was only thinking about the present.

Eventually, I got a job in a private company as a Territory Manager in sales, with a salary of ₹30,000. Our lives returned to a routine—Kaira would go to college in the morning, I would go to the office, and we would meet in the evening. During this time, I completely neglected my studies. I was just content with the job and the money it brought in. My father even gifted me a bike, making life a bit easier.

In this phase, I started imposing my will on Kaira. I would insist that we go out, eat at different places, or do something specific. Kaira once told me that being together all the time wasn't healthy and that she needed some space. This was the first time I had heard such words from her, and it made me angry. But I didn't realize at the time that she was right. I began to compare our relationship to others, which she didn't like at all. Kaira wasn't someone who just thought about herself; she wanted to bring happiness to everyone around her and didn't want to hurt anyone with her actions.

Kaira, being the kind-hearted person she was, never stopped caring for me, even when we had arguments. Whenever we fought, I would hold my head and pretend I had a severe headache, knowing that Kaira would drop everything to take care of me. She would forget her anger and start massaging my head or offering to give me medicine. Her priority was always my well-being, and seeing me in pain would make her forget any anger she had.

I knew I was taking advantage of her innocence, and it was a terrible thing to do, especially to someone like Kaira. But I continued this pattern, using the same excuse whenever we argued. If things escalated, I would even shed a few tears, knowing that it would melt her heart and she would forgive me.

I had sunk so low that I began comparing our relationship to others, something Kaira detested. She was like a Kohinoor diamond, and I was comparing her to gold and silver. Kaira wanted me to become a gentleman, someone she could be proud of and carry with dignity throughout her life. But instead of becoming her pride, I was behaving in a selfish and immature way.

Kaira had always been the one to surprise me with little things. She would make cards for me, cook special dishes, or prepare crispy corn just because I liked it. I, on the other hand, would only talk about learning to cook for her but never actually did anything. She would learn to make things from YouTube just to make me happy, while I didn't even put in half the effort she did.

As time passed, the end of our college life approached. Kaira's college was over, and now we were about to step into the real world outside. I didn't know what that world would be like—good, bad, or something else. But whatever it was, I had complete faith in Kaira. I believed that she would always be there for me, and she had even more faith in me, hoping that I would soon get a government job and take her with me.

Kaira had decided to move to Rajendra Nagar to prepare for the government exams, with a particular focus on the Staff Selection Commission (SSC) exam to become an Assistant Section Officer in the Ministry of External Affairs. Her dream was to go abroad, and this job seemed like the perfect way to fulfill that dream. She had shared her plan with me, and I, someone who didn't have any personal dreams or aspirations, agreed to join her in the same pursuit.

The very next day, I packed my bags and rented a place in the lane behind her. It wasn't because I was deeply in love with her, but because I couldn't live without her. I was selfish, as Kaira had once pointed out, and when she did, I got angry, accusing her of not recognizing the sacrifices I had made for her. But deep down, I knew she was right—I was selfish.

Once we both started coaching, Kaira was fully dedicated to her studies. She wanted us to focus entirely on our preparation, but my intentions were not the same. Kaira would get angry with me, urging me to wake up fresh in the morning, take notes properly in class, and stay focused. But my mind was elsewhere. Kaira had completely immersed herself in her studies, while I was just pretending.

Her way of studying, her method of organizing things, and her understanding of concepts were all remarkable. But I, who never really studied seriously, was only putting on a show of studying. If I had genuinely studied the way Kaira did, I might have been in a much better place today.

Kaira, with her dedication and determination, was working tirelessly to achieve her goals. She had given up her phone and cut off all distractions, focusing solely on her studies. She was determined to get out of the competition crowd and secure a good job. But my focus was nowhere near hers. I was still stuck in my old ways, thinking that just pretending to study would somehow get me through. But deep down, I knew that I was fooling myself.

Chapter 11

The day of our exam was fast approaching. I had taken exams for government jobs before, but this one was different—I had prepared thoroughly. Kaira had once told me that if I cleared this exam, it would make it easier for her to discuss our relationship with her family, who might then accept us with ease. She asked me to study not just for myself but for us, saying, "Think of it as if I'm begging you to do this for us." I realized how difficult it was for a girl to express such a thing. In my family, I had seen how a girl is expected to marry only when the guy is deemed suitable for her. And I had no such quality. Maybe, if I got the job, that would be something to my credit.

Kaira knew this too. She tried to improve me for my own good and for the sake of her family's approval. She had no personal demands—she only wanted to make sure her family was happy with her choice. But I kept telling her that my efforts weren't enough. I only wanted to do things that made me happy, not necessarily what Kaira wanted. If I truly knew Kaira, deeply and passionately, I would have done what she asked, rather than what I liked.

If I studied for eight hours a day, it was not because I couldn't live without her. I feared losing her, but I didn't have the courage to fight for it. Instead of studying 14 or 16 hours, my limit was just eight hours, and even that was a stretch. Maybe I didn't even have the ability to study those eight hours.

Finally, the day of the exam arrived. Kaira went to her exam center, and I went to mine. The results were as expected—I scored 86, while Kaira scored 114. She had prepared better than me, but luck didn't favor her, and she missed the cutoff by a few marks. I missed by a wide margin. I remembered Kaira's words: "If you pass, it will be wonderful." But in my heart, I knew that like Kalidasa, who became wise because of his wife, Kaira was worthy of being such a wife, but I wasn't worthy of being Kalidasa. When my scores were low, I was depressed, sitting with my head down. Kaira came to me, speaking softly, full of love, saying, "It's okay, we'll try again. You worked hard, and that's what matters. Don't be in a hurry, don't worry."

When I looked into her eyes, I saw fear, but she didn't want to show it to me. She was worried about what might happen if I got scared. She didn't want to cause me any pain. Her family might have been looking for a match for her, but she never mentioned it to me. Every day, she fought a new battle at home but kept me calm in front of her. Maybe I was lucky, luckier than I ever imagined, to have someone who thought only of me.

In the early days, she didn't love me as much. She entered the relationship because of something I had said, something related to her previous boyfriend. But today, I know she loves me more than anyone. She made me her entire world. We had a small, beautiful world, where we agreed that if we got a government job, we would be together. Kaira didn't want to marry. She believed that things go wrong after marriage, that the closer you are, the more problems arise. She was right—if we stayed close, we would start fighting over small things, over trivial issues.

She wanted to be with me, live in the same city, but not marry because she didn't want our life to be burdened with problems. She wanted to stay happy in her own way. If I talk about Kaira's financial situation, her father was quite wealthy and could find a suitable match for her easily. In India, it's often like this—a girl's worth is assessed, and a match is found based on that. Kaira and I both knew this very well. If she wanted, she could easily make her life beautiful in an instant. But she had made a promise to me, and nothing else mattered to her. She was ready to face any hardship with me. She knew that even if I got a government job, I wouldn't be able to give her the kind of happiness she could find elsewhere. But happiness didn't matter to her— what mattered was her love for me.

I often told Kaira that I considered her my teacher because she taught me everything—how to respect others, how to speak to people, how to show respect to elders, and how to treat women with dignity. She taught me how to behave in public places, how to behave when elders are around, always telling me to imagine how I would feel if someone treated my parents the same way. Kaira had all the qualities of a good human being.

In this world, everyone thinks only about themselves, but Kaira was the only person I met who thought about everyone else. If we parked our bike somewhere, she would always think about whether someone else's bike could get out, whether there would be space for another car. She always insisted on parking in a way that didn't inconvenience others. I would joke that she should become a parking attendant, but I knew no one thinks like that today. I felt incredibly lucky to have found a partner who cared about the world, who spoke up for it, who took a stand for it.

Kaira told me that what had to happen, happened, and now it was time for the next step. A long-distance relationship between us was about to begin. Our time in Mukherjee Nagar was coming to an end. A year had passed, and now we had to return to our respective homes. Our families felt that enough time had been spent preparing outside; now it was time to study at home without any distractions. Kaira's brother was getting married, so she went back to Kota, and I returned to Delhi to stay with my parents, as my father's job had been transferred there.

I started preparing at home, while Kaira began her preparations in Kota. The first day apart from Kaira was hard. Although we had been apart physically many times before, this time it was different because we didn't know when we would be together again. There was an uneasy restlessness, but it was inevitable. Her message reached me early in the morning: "Good morning, baby. Even though I'm far away, I'm still close to you. We'll be together soon. Just clear this exam, and then I'll be with you."

In her life, Kaira had never asked me for anything, except this one thing—to clear the exam. And if I couldn't even do that, then I would be nothing but a disgrace to myself.

CHAPTER 12

Yes, this was a new beginning for me. Kaira had said that she had complete trust in me and that if I quickly got a job, I could bring her back into my life and not just keep it long-distance. I really didn't like the idea of long-distance. Every day, seeing couples together made me wish she was with me. I wondered how she was doing, what she was up to. We could hardly talk on the phone due to our busy schedules, and messages were our only way to communicate.

I had decided that I would do whatever it took to bring her back closer. I decided to join a math coaching class to improve my chances. The coaching had started, and even though I was there, I felt lonely without Kaira. It seemed like no one was truly mine in that crowd. I kept thinking about how I would cross this crowd and become a job holder. As a middle-class person with a government officer father, I knew all the facilities would be available in Delhi, but I was worried that with my father's retirement, even those would go away. I had raised my level of study according to my means.

In the coaching center, I met a few people, including a girl. I was so serious about Kaira that I would tell anyone who asked that she is my girlfriend and that I am studying to marry her. Actually, I was very confident and proud that she was in my life, so I wanted everyone to know how lucky I was to have her. Even though she couldn't talk to me as much as she wanted, whenever she had time, she would always call me first. It seemed like she had removed everyone else from her life and made me her everything. She was very sure that she wanted to spend her whole life with me. It felt like she mentioned the job because she didn't want me to be casual about our future. She might have thought that her family had all achieved good positions, so it would be nice if her life partner also achieved something great that would make her proud in front of everyone.

But I didn't have any qualities that could make her feel proud, so maybe she wanted to find that in a job. One day, I received a call from her with a surprise. When I asked her, she lovingly told me that my sister-in-law was inviting her to New Zealand for a month. I didn't want her to leave me, but I had no option. She had never stopped me from anything before. I was worried that she might get lost in that new world, but maybe I still didn't fully understand Kaira.

When she asked me about going to the airport, she was so tired that she couldn't talk properly. So, she couldn't call me, and I felt like she didn't want to talk to me because she wanted to enjoy her trip. I was very shocked, but as soon as she reached New Zealand, even though the time zone was different, she called me daily according to that time zone, including video calls. She had dreamed of being in New Zealand, but not alone.

For me one of the biggest problems with foreign countries is using paper after using the toilet. Kaira, when she was in New Zealand, sent me a photo of the jet, showing that my problem was solved. She requested me to please bring her to New Zealand, saying that she would not ask for anything else from me in life. I said yes and started looking into how I could go there. I felt very defeated, thinking that I had nothing to fulfill her desires. But she was different; one day, she would talk about things that I was feeling at the time and then she would calm down regarding those things. She might have had her own thoughts, but she never showed them to me.

She enjoyed her time in New Zealand so much that she never made me feel like she was abroad; it was as if she was right next to me. She would share every little detail with me. She had a chance to stay for another month, but she called me and said she might not come back right now. I wanted her to come back just to meet me for 10 minutes. For me, those 10 minutes were so important that it felt like she was everything to me.

She had given up her dream of being in New Zealand and everything else just to come back and meet me. We meat only for 10 mins we went to a cafe and I promised her I will work hard and will go the New Zealand next time together. After meeting her, she went back to her home, and I returned to my place with the thought that I need to work harder so that I don't hurt someone who loves me so much.

CHAPTER 13

My entire focus was on my studies. Kaira's elder brother's wedding was taking place, and she was busy with that. She had advised me that since this time my studies were not going well, I should take up a job so that we could get settled, and she would handle it next time. I confidently told her that my preparation was good and there was no need to worry; it would be fine. She was waiting with hope. She had invited me to the wedding, but considering my situation, I wasn't in a position to attend. I didn't have a decent job or anything; she had invited me, I wish I would have had to explain who I was. What she will say about me to her family. He is my boyfriend, with whom I wanted to spend my life, was not even worth two pennies. I had considered him my everything, but he couldn't even manage a small job. The wedding concluded, and exactly two months later, my exam was approaching. Despite preparing well according to my ability and competition level, I still wasn't at a good standing. I didn't have the qualification I needed. As a result, my exam didn't go well. Kaira also didn't do well this time; both of us ended up in the same condition as before. Neither I had a job, nor did Kaira.

But when a girl loves you, she leaves everything and focuses only on you. She did just that. She put everything aside and focused on me, even though my exam didn't go well. According to her, if this exam didn't work out, it would cause problems in our being together, but her heart was with me. She said our strategy might not have been correct, but she always want me to be at good position. After not performing well in exam. She tried to calm me by saying we shouldn't be disheartened. We should try again and work hard this time, and it will work out. She told me not to worry and to make a good strategy this time.

I understood that she was talking about a job to make me a better person and to improve my situation, but she loved me sincerely and couldn't think of being with anyone else. I also knew that in front of Kaira, I was not worthy. She deserved a much better person, and if I wanted to give her a good life, I had to get a job. I had become fearful of SSC completion and was now looking towards other exams, hoping to get into a government job.

Kaira was very dedicated, completely focused on SSC and did not give as much importance to other jobs. We always disagreed on this point, but as a serious aspirant, she was right. As the next exam approached, I met Kaira a couple of times—once in Delhi and once in Jaipur. Both times, I saw a kind of fear in her eyes. For someone who is pursuing a government job, the process is so tough and slow that it often feels like we are left behind, while others progress.

She hugged me and started crying. When I asked her the reason, she said she didn't know but just felt like crying. I felt that she might be suffering from depression and that I was the cause. Kaira's former roommate was getting married to a guy from a very wealthy business family; it was a luxurious wedding. Kaira also deserved something like that, but her current condition was due to a mistake she made on April 16, 2015, which led to her current situation. I sincerely wanted to do something great for her and even thought about opening a coaching institute to start teaching and perhaps gain some recognition and money.

If you want to achieve something great, you need to focus on a single goal. My attention was scattered, and that was my weakness. This was going to be our third attempt; by now, we should have secured a selection. My exam center was in Delhi, and Kaira's was in Kota. She was more worried about my exam than her own. Despite her own preparation, she would constantly ask me about my preparation and if I was studying well. She wanted to make sure I wouldn't be nervous before the exam and even sent me motivational videos and messages to keep me encouraged.

Honestly, this time I was scared, fearing that I might lose Kaira. This fear was drowning me. She had told me that her father was looking for an IAS match for her and would find one, so I should at least secure a level 7 job in SSC to give her family something to say. I understood her situation well. My father was an officer in a bank, and even he got married because of his job in mind. No girl's family would accept a road-side man for marriage. Kaira's family had always been supportive of her. They had never denied her anything and she never wanted to cause them any trouble. She held her family in the highest regard.

I feared that if her family opposed our marriage, she wouldn't be able to take a stand. Though Kaira never made me feel this way, I still felt it. The day of my exam arrived, and I messed up the paper. I couldn't complete it. When I came out, there were 10 missed calls from Kaira. She was eagerly waiting, hoping for good news about my paper. When I told her that the paper wasn't completed, she was very disappointed, as if her own exam worries were secondary. She had given up immediately, even though she had never seen herself above me.

Perhaps true love is when someone is happier with your success than with their own. She always wanted me to do better, even though she had more capability. This is a trait often seen in Indian women—they want their husbands to be their pride. By failing the third time, I had broken her pride. That night, she called me, very frustrated, saying she couldn't be with me anymore. She was done with me. It seemed like her frustration was speaking, and she said she couldn't talk to me anymore. She had wanted something from me, and I couldn't deliver. I was failing from the pre-exam stage itself, and mains were far off. Forget top ranks; I wasn't even making it among 150,000 candidates.

I tried to convince her that I would become successful within three months, but in her anger, she didn't believe it. She had no faith in it; it wasn't a plausible outcome. Someone who hadn't done anything in three years would not suddenly achieve success. She hadn't blocked me but refused to talk to me. After that, the next day, she called me regarding some work, which had nothing to do with the job. She was only concerned about me, and I knew that.

But I also knew that she was no longer serious about her exam. She had filled out the form, so she went to give the exam, but otherwise, she was not serious about it. From this, you can gauge how deeply she loved me. My poor performance in the exam meant nothing compared to her own exam. She had worked so hard and wanted so badly for her exam to clear.

CHAPTER 14

My entire world had fallen apart, and the one responsible for it was none other than me. If I had put in the right effort on time, perhaps she would have been with me today. This thought kept me awake at night; for years, I had lost the habit of sleeping without hearing "good morning" and "good night." I used to sleep early at night but didn't feel like waking up in the morning. If I did wake up, it felt like I wouldn't be able to handle the whole day.

I didn't know how to live without her; dying seemed easier than living a day without sharing everything with her. I couldn't even be angry with God because He had given me three chances, and I hadn't cleared any of them. I felt defeated in life. I didn't even know where my life was heading. Sometimes I looked at the syllabus for a bank PO, and other times at the GMAT. My only goal was to bring Kaira back, but I couldn't figure out how that would be possible. I didn't even know how her exams had gone; she hadn't shared that with me.

Day and night, I only wished for her to come back. I spent about 4-5 nights without her, during which I had called her twice. Then one night, I received a call asking me to send a number for a PG (paying guest accommodation). I was completely shocked, not understanding what was happening. Before I could grasp the situation, the next line was that she was coming to Indirapuram the next day to look at PGs. I was overjoyed, but I was also unkempt with a scruffy beard. With great effort, I went to get her from the metro. She arrived wearing a pink shirt and blue jeans, holding a book.

We saw many rooms with the help of a boy who worked at my place, and she liked one of them. I was constantly thinking, "Just let her come here, and everything will be great." She came, but her anger didn't disappear immediately. Her brother brought her some things, and I wanted to do everything for her. However, after she arrived, I called her and requested to meet, but she immediately refused, saying she was there to study. If I continued like this, she would move out. I was happy that she was at least with me, but Kaira is very soft-hearted, and within 2-3 days, her anger subsided. I didn't know that I was about to enjoy the best phase of my life. Spending time together, going to the library, having lunch, and being together made me feel like all my sorrows were gone in a moment.

Kaira's plan was for us to join the library together and give our preparation a fresh start. She didn't have any hope from her previous results, and my exam had gone badly. Kaira wanted us to work hard day and night. But on the other hand, I felt that since Kaira was with me, I should enjoy every moment with her. We did join the library, but I distracted her more than I let her study. Sometimes I would suggest going out, and my distractions affected her concentration.

She had problems with the cold; the exam was in January. Because of the cold, she woke up late, and I blamed the cold for not being able to study, requesting God not to have exams in the cold in the future. Life requires a good partner who, even if you don't feel like doing something, will make sure you get it done for your own good, without just indulging you. I did this with Kaira.

When the exam day came, her family took her to Kota, where the exam center was. She started the exam, but due to insufficient preparation, it didn't go well. We both started preparing for the next CGL exam with the thought of giving our best. Kaira knew that I was a distraction in her life. She even tried to suggest that we join separate libraries, but I was adamant about staying together. I wasn't thinking about the future; I only saw that I couldn't live without her, so I didn't want to be away from her.

A wise person might have changed the library, focused on preparation, and planned to spend the rest of their life with Kaira.

Chapter 15

The problem was that I lacked confidence in my life, and it reflected in my personality as well. On the other hand, she (Kaira) was completely serious about her goals, but I kept planting negative thoughts in her mind, like we should have a backup option other than SSC CGL. For a serious aspirant like her, the only backup option seemed to be banking preparation. I told her, "Let's first secure a job as a bank PO, and then we can continue preparing for SSC." She agreed, though she was slightly doubtful at first, but eventually, she came around to my suggestion. Maybe she trusted me so much that she would believe what I said immediately, or if not right away, after some time.

She used to say that in our relationship, it's always been my decisions that prevailed. I would reply that I was following her lead, but in truth, it was mostly my way. She would always agree to what I said and never went against my wishes. Early in our relationship, I gave her cards and gifts, but she would make me paintings, write letters, or cook something special for me. She knew I loved crispy corn, so she learned to make it at home just for me.

I didn't reciprocate in the same way, though. My only constant gesture was waiting for her near her home; she knew I loved her, but perhaps I wasn't able to express it as truly as she did. Real love was what she showed me. I would often go to her place, where she lived on the top floor, enduring the heat and humidity, but she stayed there just to be near me. She could have moved to a more comfortable place, like one of her brothers' homes, but she chose to stay close to me, bearing all the hardships with a smile on her face. Despite everything, she managed everything perfectly without any complaints. She always had a smile on her face.

Even though I suggested she should get something installed in her home to make it more comfortable, she never wanted to burden her father with expenses. Instead, she even started tutoring to manage her own expenses, so she wouldn't be a burden on her family. Meanwhile, I was only living off my parents' money, with no real pressure or responsibility on me. She was the one who was struggling for every little thing, yet she prepared much better for the exams than I did.

Sometimes she would ask me to name any quality in me that she could rely on to trust me and stay with me. At those moments, I would remain silent because I couldn't think of any. I hadn't kept any promises I made to her, yet she stayed with me because she loved me. But even trust has its limits, and I kept pushing the boundaries. I believed that love was enough, but in reality, life is not just about love; you have to do something to make it work, and I wasn't able to do that.

The only thing she ever asked of me was to secure a good job so that we could have a stable life. She didn't ask for much. She knew that for us to build a life together, financial stability was crucial, and she was working hard for it. I, on the other hand, wasn't making the necessary efforts.

Eventually, we shifted our focus to banking exams. We started preparing diligently, but just as we were getting into the rhythm, SSC announced a huge recruitment drive with 36,000 vacancies. I convinced her to switch back to SSC preparation, believing it was a rare opportunity we couldn't miss. This constant back-and-forth in our plans was my doing, and it disrupted our focus. Changing from one exam pattern to another was difficult, and it affected our preparation.

Despite the struggles, we started preparing for SSC again, putting in long hours at the library. We would reach the library early in the morning and stay until late at night. We motivated each other, discussing questions over cups of tea at our favorite stall. When you have someone to walk the difficult path with, life becomes a lot easier, and the destination seems closer. It felt like we were on the brink of achieving our goal.

When the exam day arrived, we both cleared the preliminary exam, which boosted our confidence. We threw ourselves into preparing for the mains exam with renewed determination. Her scores were always better than mine, which often made me anxious, but she would comfort me, saying it's okay, and would even sit with me for hours, analyzing my mistakes and helping me improve.

The day of the mains exam finally came. Unfortunately, during her exam, her computer system hung for about 10 minutes, which is a significant loss of time in a competitive exam. In the rush to catch up, she made some mistakes. It was a twist of fate because her selection was almost certain otherwise. On the other hand, my exam went smoothly, but my preparation wasn't as strong, and I didn't make it past the final selection. If not for the technical issue, she would have definitely been selected.

We endured this setback and decided to give it one last shot before considering other options. Meanwhile, I had been appearing for various other exams, including the railway exam. When my railway prelims result came out, I had cleared it. Kaira advised me that it wasn't a great job and that I should focus on SSC. She was right, but I was too insecure about my capabilities and wanted to secure any job I could, even if it wasn't the best.

Kaira's advice was sound; focusing on the railway exam affected my SSC preparation. But I was adamant about securing the railway job, believing that any job would provide some financial stability. However, I didn't realize that true financial stability comes from being financially independent, not from a low-paying job that still leaves you dependent on your parents.

I went ahead and cleared the railway mains exam, and now the final stage was the psychometric test for the position of station master. Kaira insisted on accompanying me to Mumbai for the test. This was the first time she traveled without a confirmed ticket, and when we managed to reach Mumbai, we felt like we had accomplished something big.

In Mumbai, we stayed in a hotel. Kaira was there to support me, giving me the strength to face the exam. On the way, we even met one of my favorite actors, Vinay Pathak. Kaira confidently approached him and requested a photo with me, calling me "her man" with such pride and assurance that I felt like we were already married. That line echoed in my mind as I kept looking at the photo later.

During the exam, Kaira stayed with me, helping me practice and guiding me through the questions. She even wanted to drop me off at the exam center in the morning, but I managed to convince her to pick me up afterward instead. After the exam, she picked me up, and we visited the Siddhivinayak Temple. We explored Mumbai, and she loved the city so much that we made a plan to visit every year.

Returning to Delhi, we resumed our preparation, but I was anxiously waiting for my railway exam result, hoping it would give me a job and some stability.

Chapter 16

"This was a significant disappointment for me—the results came out, and I failed in the psychometric test. I wasn't selected. Both Kaira and I were very disheartened. Rani had bought a cardholder for me, intending to give it to me when I got the job, but she didn't. She hid it in her cupboard. A few days later, when I asked about it, she said she was thinking of giving it to a friend for their birthday. I accepted it, but little did I know she had kept it for me as a gift if I had been selected.

Kaira and I used to walk along the road, discussing what we would buy after securing jobs—a car, perhaps—but it wasn't meant to be. We both prepared diligently, and while studying, we supported each other, which kept us strong. Many people were in dire straits, but the companionship we shared made our lives content; we never felt lacking in anything. A significant factor in this was the support from my family. Financially, I wasn't under much strain because my father had a government job, so he provided for all our needs. Kaira's father also had a government job and was a very self-respecting person, so Kaira never asked him for more money than necessary. She earned the rest by giving tuitions.

If anyone had asked me, I would have said that I wanted to spend my entire life with Kaira. She was someone who thought of everyone, and though she lived in a flat, she never allowed me to visit her home, which used to bother me. I would ask her, 'Can't I ever come to your place?' But when I thought deeply, I realized she did it out of concern for what her neighbors might think. She was very aware of her dignity and boundaries. If someone questioned her character, she knew she should first reflect on her own conduct. In this regard, her character was as pure and simple as Sita from the Ramayana. She enjoyed good food and good clothing but never indulged in unnecessary expenses. Unlike many girlfriends who spend lavishly, Kaira never asked me to spend money on her. We maintained a balanced approach, sharing the expenses evenly.

Our chances of selection were increasing. I cleared the first round of the CGL exam, and Kaira passed two. Alongside the CGL, I cleared the Railway and CHSL exams. I was working hard on my typing skills, with Kaira constantly encouraging me. She always reassured me, saying, 'Don't worry, you'll succeed. I swear you will.' Her motivation meant everything to me, but I sometimes felt anxious, which hindered my performance.

When I went for the CHSL typing test, I failed—I just couldn't manage it, despite trying my best. As exams came and went, there was hope that I might succeed somewhere, but I kept failing at the final stages. Still, I was grateful that I was close to success and that Kaira and I were mentally strong. To keep our spirits high, we started using the society gym and swimming pool together. We lived a beautiful life, a life so beautiful that many people can only dream of it.

When my birthday came around, I would be demanding, saying, 'I'm the birthday boy, do this for me, do that for me,' and she would do everything with a smile. She planned everything meticulously, even taking me to stand-up comedy shows. Though I sometimes complained that it wasn't fun, she tolerated my whims because it was my birthday. She endured all my tantrums, yet another exam result was approaching—this time, a

Railway post. I had cleared the exam, and the next stage was typing. With God's blessing and Kaira's love, I cleared the exam, but the final hurdle was typing.

I began typing practice with the determination that I had to secure this job at any cost. I put my heart and soul into it, practicing every day. I remember calling Kaira after every exam, and she would always say, 'Don't worry, you'll clear it.' When the result came, and I passed, we celebrated with a small party. Such little celebrations were big for us.

The next step was to wait for the merit list, which would determine my selection. Months passed as we anxiously awaited the result. When the result finally came, my name wasn't on it. I was devastated, but Kaira knew how to pick up the pieces. She comforted me, saying, 'Don't worry, I'm with you. Even if we have nothing, as long as we're together, we have everything.' Those words meant the world to me, and they lifted my spirits. We started preparing for the next exam with renewed energy.

Months passed, and I was still hoping that my name might appear on the waiting list, as I had missed the cutoff by just 0.5 marks. Meanwhile, Kaira was also preparing intensely. Her presence in my life was everything to me—without her, I wouldn't have been able to sustain myself. She was my strength, and without her, I couldn't imagine living. I couldn't achieve anything without her.

At one point, someone suggested that I start observing fasts on Tuesdays and even consulted a priest about my horoscope. Kaira and I even matched our horoscopes to see if we were compatible. All this effort made me realize that I could never find anyone better than Kaira, and I was determined to keep her in my life, no matter what. I knew that I wasn't good enough for her and that she could have anyone she wanted.

In the end, Kaira was the best for me, and I was the worst for her. Despite all the challenges and the heartbreaks, I was always sure that I wanted to spend my life with her. I knew that no matter how many times I failed, Kaira would always be there to support me, and that was all I needed to keep going.

Chapter 17

In the grand tapestry of life, God's plan often includes delays, but promises of good things to come. This was evident in my life as I waited for days on end to see the railway waiting list. When it was finally published, my name was there. It was a moment I had been eagerly anticipating. As I was on my way home, I received the news while waiting outside the metro station on my scooter, preparing to pick up someone and head home together.

Excitement bubbled within me as I reached the station and immediately informed Kaira about the results. Though I was thrilled that my name appeared on the list, the actual list wasn't opening yet. Kaira, ever the voice of reason, advised me not to get my hopes up too high, fearing that if the list revealed otherwise, I might struggle with the disappointment.

A few days earlier, we had watched the movie *Barbie*, featuring the story of Manoj and Shraddha. In the film, Shraddha supported Manoj at every turn. In my life, Kaira was my Shraddha, standing by me in every possible way. Though I didn't see myself as remarkable as Manoj, Kaira had an immense impact on my life.

Arriving at her house, we set about checking the results. When we saw my name on the list, Kaira's eyes welled with tears. Despite her best efforts to conceal her emotions, her joy and relief were palpable as she silently cried.

The job with the Government of India was secured, and we knew that hard work lay ahead. While the job was not Kaira's ultimate goal, she was clear about her ambitions, always aiming for the best opportunities. For me, it was a small step—a means to free my mind for future endeavors. I believed that this job would provide the peace of mind needed to prepare for bigger challenges.

Our confidence soared, and that night, we celebrated at Barbeque Nation. As we enjoyed our meal, Kaira playfully teased me about becoming a Government of India employee. Her teasing brought me immense happiness, though I reminded her to wait until the medical examination was complete before celebrating too much.

Kaira, a late-night movie enthusiast, often watched films past 11 PM, a habit I struggled to keep up with. No matter how hard I tried, I'd begin to doze off as soon as the movie started. I joked that being with her made me so comfortable that sleep was inevitable. Kaira didn't fully understand, but I explained that her presence made me feel at ease, providing a sense of safety that led to peaceful sleep.

Two days before the medical examination, scheduled for January 22nd, anxiety began to grip me. To calm my nerves, I had all my tests done. Everything was normal except for a slightly elevated blood pressure of 150. The doctor attributed it to nervousness and reassured me not to worry.

To distract myself, Kaira and I planned a trip to Khatu Shyam Ji, a destination she loved for its adventure. During our drive back, I wanted to avoid risky situations, but Kaira, eager for adventure, suggested following a bus through the fog. Scared, I opted for caution and parked at a nearby hotel for the night.

At the hotel, the room rent was 1200 rupees. Kaira had advised me to negotiate for 800, but when the hotel quoted 1000, I knew Kaira wouldn't approve. So, I claimed the rate was 800. However, when I paid via scanner, the speaker audibly confirmed 1000 rupees. Kaira, who despises dishonesty, warned me to abandon this habit. Though I had a tendency to lie, I promised to improve. Despite her annoyance, Kaira's trust in me meant she forgave me.

As the medical exam approached, my anxiety about my blood pressure increased. A doctor prescribed medication, but it only worsened my condition, raising my blood pressure to 170, and eventually, 200. Fearful it might be my last night, I called Kaira, who stayed on the line all night, listening to my labored breathing.

By 4 AM, my condition worsened, and my father and I rushed to the hospital. The doctor confirmed my blood pressure was dangerously high but gradually stabilized after treatment. Kaira called multiple times, and when my mother answered, she expressed worry and guilt. Kaira, devastated by the news, cried upon learning that my mother blamed herself.

I felt compelled to apologize to Kaira, as the trip had been my idea. Despite her initial suggestion of a shorter trip, I had insisted on an eight-hour journey. Nonetheless, Kaira put her feelings aside and stayed by my side in the hospital.

After being discharged, I prepared for the medical exam in Ahmedabad. My father's support was invaluable, and Kaira remained available by phone, encouraging me to focus on the exam. Despite my fear that my elevated blood pressure might disqualify me, Kaira's words (know matter what is the condition I will be with you) and belief were comforting. The next day, my blood pressure was normal, and I received a fit certificate, ready to join my first government job.

Although I was reluctant to start immediately, fearing a posting in Gujarat, Kaira encouraged me to proceed, knowing it would give me time to prepare for better opportunities. Her practical approach prioritized our future over her own convenience.

My posting in Baroda was confirmed, and Kaira accompanied me on my first journey there as I don't want to go there alone. We arrived on March 8th, marking the start of a new chapter. We checked into a hotel, and the next morning, Kaira woke me up, saying, "It's your first day at the office." Like a parent dropping off their child, she accompanied me to the office.

In the evening, we visited a temple to offer our prayers, and then explored local Gujarati snacks like khaman and dhokla. Our days felt like a newlywed couple's—simple, yet filled with joy. However, the impending return of Kaira to Delhi left me anxious and lonely, missing her presence deeply.

Two weeks later, Kaira returned to Delhi, and the separation was painful. The emptiness of being alone in a place we had shared was overwhelming. I longed for the day we would be reunited, cherishing the moments we had together and anticipating our future.

Chapter 18

Every Morning Began with Her

My day revolved around a single phone call. Just a call, where my words would bridge the distance between us. Every morning, as I got ready for work, the first thing I did was to call her, waking her up with a gentle "Good Morning." She'd often ask for just half an hour more, and I'd smile, saying, "Alright, take 45 minutes." After that, I'd call her again, asking, "Is my little one up now?"

Once she was awake, I'd tell her to freshen up and give me a call before heading to the library. Where she was in life, she had to go alone, a burden that weighed heavily on her, yet she never let it show in her voice or her words. Perhaps, it was because I never gave her a chance to feel alone, always reminding her how I couldn't live without her, how everything felt incomplete, and how I couldn't focus on anything without her.

Our Love was My Strength

My lunch break was at 1:30 PM, and I'd ask if she was eating, what she was having, and how her studies were going. I always reminded her that her priority was her studies, urging her not to lose focus. She wanted me to become a successful officer, not just for herself, but for both of us, and more so, for me. She desired that I hold a respectable position, a symbol of pride and honor.

Just like I had always wished for my father's success and promotions, I never felt greed for any material gain. I simply wanted to be able to say, "My father retired from such a high post." Perhaps she wanted the same, to feel proud and say, "He's my man." I knew she was already proud of me, but she wanted more reasons to feel that pride.

A Love Beyond Measure

One day, during a call, I was frustrated with my work, unable to find time to study. She noticed my distress and said, "Listen, if you can't manage to study now, we'll find a solution." I snapped a little, "What should I do? I can't handle everything at once. You told me to take up this job, and now I can't keep up with it. What should I do?" She calmly responded, "You'll have to do whatever it takes, you know that. Let's make a deal: I'll study hard this time, and once I succeed, you can quit your job and focus on your studies."

Hearing this, my eyes filled with tears. It struck me how rare it is to find someone like her, and how incredibly lucky I was to have her in my life.

The Little Moments We Cherished

Every weekend, I would visit Delhi, where we used to roam around in the rain, reminiscing about the times we spent together, visiting the library, enjoying each other's company. Those were our happiest moments, and though we were apart, phone calls, especially audio calls, kept us close. She didn't like video calls much, but I'd insist, just to tease her and see how she reacted. However, she found more joy in our long conversations over audio calls, where we'd share our little moments.

Our life was filled with happiness, and we were deeply content in each other's presence. I would often pray that no evil eye would ever cast a shadow on our relationship. She visited the temple daily, asking the divine for just one thing: to keep us together, as that bond was the most important part of our lives.

Dreams of Togetherness

Everywhere I went, I dreamed of the day she would join me. I planned all our future moments together, from visiting Pavagadh to simply walking hand in hand through the places we loved. In every plan, every thought, she was there. In truth, for the past nine years, my life has revolved entirely around her.

I made some friends along the way, but I couldn't sleep until I'd spoken to her at night. Without her, I am incomplete.

Chapter 19

A Chaotic Day and an Unexpected Turn

Today was one of those days when nothing seemed to go right. The power was out, and with it, the Wi-Fi. Even the AC, which I had recently installed, was out of order due to a gas issue. Frustrated with everything, I thought about joining a library where I could study on Saturdays and Sundays, or perhaps even drop by for a bit in the mornings and evenings. I shared this thought with Kaira, and she calmly replied, "Yes, go ahead, join a library. It might help you escape the chaos at home and give you a better environment to study."

After this I felt my breath quicken, my heart race. Suddenly, I was overwhelmed with a sense of panic, as if I had committed some grave mistake. The person who had been listening to me intently was taken aback, asking anxiously, "What happened? What's wrong?"

He couldn't understand what had triggered this response in me. Despite his own troubles, he was listening to me carefully, almost as if he was deeply interested in what I was saying. But seeing me in this state, he couldn't bear it any longer. Not knowing what else to do, he dialed 108—the emergency ambulance service.

When I opened my eyes, I found myself lying in an ambulance, speeding towards the hospital. I was later placed in a bed in the general ward, surrounded by people crying out in pain, each one grappling with their own suffering. They had given me some kind of injection—likely a sedative—because I felt drowsy, unaware of how much time had passed or where I exactly was.

As I slowly regained consciousness, I saw the person I had been speaking to earlier standing by my side. He looked worried, asking, "What happened to you? Just moments ago, you were telling me such a happy love story, and now this… What went wrong?"

I tried to reassure him, "Nothing, nothing… just a momentary problem." But even as I spoke, I couldn't shake off the guilt. Nearby, there had been an accident case, and the police were present. I suddenly started walking towards them, pleading, "Please save me, I've committed a crime! I'm guilty, and I need to be punished!"

The police, looking bewildered, dismissed me as a madman, irritated that they had to deal with such nonsense while on duty. Frustrated, I returned to my bed, where a doctor came over to check on me. He asked, "What's wrong with you?"

I replied, "Nothing… I've just been going through some tough times. But it's nothing that serious, just a moment of weakness. I wanted to end it, but this fool didn't let me." I pointed to the person standing by my side.

The doctor looked at both of us, then spoke calmly, "You're fine. You just had a panic attack." He handed me some medicine and told me to wait outside. But when I tried to leave, they wouldn't let me go, citing hospital rules. "You can't just leave like this; we'll have to file a case against you if you do," they warned.

Feeling trapped, I tried to reason with them, asking them to at least allow me to atone for my mistakes. But they wouldn't listen. Instead, they gave me another injection—likely another sedative. When I opened my eyes again, I was in a doctor's room. The doctor, who seemed to be a psychiatrist, smiled gently at me and said, "Good morning, Mr. Pathak. How are you feeling?"

I replied, "Sir, I just want to go home. Please, let me go home."

He offered me a cup of coffee and said, "Why don't you have a cup of coffee with me first? Then let's talk." The nameplate on his desk read 'Dr. Jain.' He looked at me kindly and asked, "What's troubling you? You can talk to me. We can work things out together. There's no need to take such drastic steps."

His calm demeanor and warm smile brought a sense of peace, as if everything might just be okay after all.

Chapter 20

I was in no position to speak. My mind was overwhelmed with anxiety, and I was struggling to find a way to fix things before nightfall. I stared blankly at the wall, unable to articulate the turmoil within me. The doctor, sensing my distress, said, "If you don't share what's troubling you, we can't begin to address it. Start by giving me some insight into what's happening, and then we'll work together to find a solution. Speak calmly and openly."

I wasn't sure what the doctor had given me to drink, but it made me feel strangely light, as though the weight of the world had been lifted off my shoulders. It was then that I felt able to speak. I turned towards him and said, "Doctor, I've committed a crime, but I'm not being punished for it, and that's what's tormenting me the most."

The doctor inquired gently, "What crime have you committed? Please tell me about it." I replied, "I betrayed someone's trust—someone who saw me as their entire world. I betrayed their faith."

Recognizing the gravity of my emotional state, the doctor asked, "Did you betray your girlfriend?" I corrected him, "She wasn't just my girlfriend; she was my fiancée. She had gone through immense lengths to make our relationship known—convincing her mother to approve of our marriage, informing her brother and sister-in-law, and eventually, everyone else. She had sent my photos to her home; everything was set for our wedding. Our life was moving smoothly towards a happy future. But then, Doctor, I panicked and made a grave mistake."

The doctor probed further, "It takes two to create a situation like this. Was there something lacking on your part, or perhaps something missing from her side?" I quickly countered, "No, she never did anything wrong. If her only mistake was trusting me too much and loving me unconditionally, then that's on me. She sacrificed her freedom and liberty for me, and if that was her mistake, then so be it. But I refuse to hear a word against her. Anyone who dares to speak ill of her will have to answer to me."

My voice trembled with anger. The doctor, recognizing the depth of my feelings, said, "Suresh shared part of your story with me. I will do my best to help bring Kaira back into your life." Overwhelmed with emotion, I was crying and laughing simultaneously, expressing my gratitude. "Thank you, Doctor. I will tell you everything, but please, bring Kaira back into my life."

"I once went to a library and saw a girl sitting there. She glanced at me, and I at her, but we didn't speak. After a while, she asked if I'd like to have tea with her. I agreed, and that was our first conversation. We began sharing details about ourselves. I told her I worked for the Ministry of Railways in Baroda. She revealed she was a doctor. I had also aspired to become a doctor after high school but never succeeded. We talked for a while before parting ways."

"That night, I told Kaira, my fiancée, about the girl, saying she had shown interest in me. Kaira didn't take it seriously, dismissing it as overthinking. 'Just because a girl talks to you doesn't mean she's interested,' she said. I knew she was right, but a part of me was intrigued by the girl's attention. Kaira called me narcissistic, and we ended the conversation."

"The next day, I went back to the library and saw the girl again. We exchanged greetings, and she invited me for tea once more. This time, she was with friends—Rinki, Tushar, and Mahesh. They spoke in Gujarati, which I didn't understand fully, but I listened. I had been spending a lot of time on the phone with Kaira, my only companion, and felt increasingly comfortable with Rinki and her friends."

"During one of our tea outings, Rinki asked if I was single or in a relationship. Habitually, I said I was in a relationship. But that day, an impulse overcame me, urging me to say I was single. I'm deeply sorry, Kaira. I will carry this burden to my grave. I should have shown her a picture of you, my fiancée, but I didn't. That was the beginning of my betrayal. It was a huge mistake, and I knew it."

"Rinki and I continued to spend time together, and our interactions grew closer in ways they shouldn't have. I was crossing boundaries and breaking my commitment to Kaira. I knew it was wrong but couldn't stop myself."

"On my birthday, Kaira visited me, planning to make it special as she always did. I told Rinki about Kaira's visit and asked her not to contact me for a few days. Kaira arrived, and I picked her up from the railway station. As soon as I saw her, I was overwhelmed with guilt. I felt so ashamed that I couldn't even greet her properly."

"At home, she admired the house, but I was tormented by my betrayal. The next morning, Kaira checked my phone and discovered all the messages between Rinki and me. She couldn't believe what she saw. I was unable to speak in front of the psychiatrist and fainted."

Chapter 21

A few hours later, I awoke to find a psychiatrist standing before me, gently assuring me, "Don't worry, Gautam; things will be okay." Her words were precisely what I needed to hear, yet they mirrored the reality I had been dreading. Kaira had reached a breaking point; the thought of staying in that house any longer was unbearable for her. She had never looked at another man, never spoken to anyone else, nor did she harbor thoughts of anyone but me. I was her world, and now, I had shattered it.

I had filled her life with so much of my presence that I had inadvertently shut out everyone else. Her deep trust in me made my betrayal even more profound. When she chose to leave, it was clear she couldn't stay any longer. Without hesitation, Kaira gathered her belongings and left. Despite my desperate attempts to stop her, my pleas fell on deaf ears. She walked resolutely toward her own home.

For so long, I had been the sole person in her life, and seeing her shoulder all those responsibilities alone brought tears to my eyes. The monster within me still roared, convincing me that I couldn't survive without Kaira. I reached out to Rinki, explaining that Kaira had discovered everything about us and that I was frantically searching for her, hoping to bring her back. My heart was heavy with the fear that she might never return. I told myself it was fine, but deep down, I was crumbling. I searched for Kaira everywhere, enduring immense suffering, until I finally found her at the airport. But when I approached her, she refused to speak or even look at me, huddled quietly in a corner.

Despite my desperate attempts to reach her, Kaira remained unresponsive. I knew I had inflicted deep wounds, leaving her emotionally shattered. She was so broken that she could barely comprehend the extent of my actions. In her agony, Kaira moved to Delhi, and I followed her. At the airport, she asked me to contact Rinki. While Kaira spoke with Rinki, I still kept Rinki as a backup, fearing that if Kaira left me, I might spiral into madness without her.

That same night, Kaira called me, her voice trembling with despair. She cried uncontrollably, saying, "My chest hurts." I promised her I would forsake everything and rush to her side. Through her tears, she lamented how I had destroyed our relationship, saying, "You broke my pride, my trust." I vowed to leave Rinki and ensure no one else would be in my life but her.

That night, as I rested my head on her lap, I promised that no one would come between us. I sent a message to Rinki, ending our relationship and making it clear that there was no room for anyone else in my life. But the sins of the past do not vanish easily. The next morning, Rinki called to reveal truths Kaira hadn't known. She disclosed that I had lied about my relationship with Kaira and mentioned our physical bond.

Kaira was devastated upon hearing this. The revelation shattered her further, and she demanded I leave her life. Overwhelmed by the fear of not surviving alone, I told her I would ask Rinki to return if she left me. Her response was cold: "Just get lost."

I left Kaira's house feeling as though I had committed a grave crime. The realization of my actions weighed heavily on me. I needed help to recover from this emotional turmoil, someone to stabilize my mental state. Despite thinking that

Rinki might be a support, things only worsened. No one can ever take Kaira's place in my life

As I walked away from Kaira's house, I was struck by the familiar places—the circle where I used to pick her up, the gate where I used to wait. My mother had prepared food that night and brought it to me. As we ate together, my mother, who knew the truth about my relationship with Kaira, pretended ignorance. She told Kaira she thought we were merely friends and that she was unaware of our plans to marry.

I had always been open with my mother about my love for Kaira and my desire to marry her, but my fears about her family's acceptance due to my financial instability led me to keep certain truths hidden. My mother's distorted version of events only compounded Kaira's heartbreak. She felt betrayed not only by me but by my family as well. I felt like a murderer, tormented by the guilt of destroying everything that mattered to me. The pain was so intense that I wished for death over enduring this suffering. My family, who had been told of my love for Kaira, had destroyed everything.

Kaira's family, while recognizing my mistakes, treated me with respect. Her brother told me that forgiveness was solely Kaira's decision and that they could not force her to forgive me. The contrast between Kaira's forgiving family and my own, who seemed only to know blame, was striking.

That night, I returned home, unable to sleep alone, and spent the night with my father, consumed by fear and loneliness.

On June 23rd, I was desperate to reconcile with Kaira. I hoped that Rinki might help persuade her to return. I had asked Rinki to block me everywhere, which she did. I contacted Tushar, a mutual friend, asking him to tell Rinki to contact me she messaged me. I asked her to reach out to Kaira and tell her the truth she might believe you. She agreed and promised to assist.

A few days later, Rinki reached out and want to meet. I clearly said I could manage a video call, as my mental state was too fragile for a face-to-face encounter. That call marked the end of our interactions.

Since then, I have been waiting for Kaira, seeing her in every corner and yearning to speak with her. Her absence haunts me, and I can't escape the longing to be with her once more.

Chapter 22

Now it was time for my questions and answers. The doctor had listened to everything and was looking at me very carefully. He said, "Look, if you were a criminal, you wouldn't be in this condition. You've committed a crime, but you're suffering, tormented by the realization of your wrongdoing. I can see that, and because of your condition, I'm willing to help you. Quietly write a letter to kaira, and in it, ask her for four months. In these four months, do as much good as you can to make up for your mistakes. Tell her that after these four months, she should meet with you. If she agrees to meet you after these four months, then show her all the good deeds you've done. If she feels she can trust you again, maybe she'll give you another chance. And if she does, it'll be the best thing that can happen to you. Focus on doing good things, so that when you meet her on December 8th, she might feel like giving you another chance.

On December 8th, 2024, your life will be decided. Until then, do as many good things as you can, and I'll pray to God for you." He gave me three or four medicines and wrote down instructions, saying, "Only take these medicines if you really need them. If bad thoughts come to you, take the medicine. And if you still can't control them, you must call me immediately. You have to promise me that." After securing my promise and trust, the doctor sent me home.

When I stepped outside, Suresh had heard everything. I asked Suresh, "Suresh Bhai, you've heard my entire story, but you haven't told me anything about yourself. You must have your own troubles, which is why you sit outside the station every night drinking. Tell me."

Suresh looked at me and said, "You're battling your own pain. You're not ready to hear about someone else's sorrow. On December 8th, when everything turns out well for you, I'll tell you my story. Let's meet on December 8th." Suresh said this, and I thought that maybe on December 8th, I'll write another book. The title will be *From This Life to the Next.*